MICHELLE OBAMA

QUOTES TO LIVE BY

CARLTON
BOOKS

THIS IS A CARLTON BOOK

Published in 2019 by Carlton Books
An imprint of the Carlton Publishing Group
20 Mortimer Street
London W1T 3JW

Editor: Alex Lemon
Designer: Lucy Palmer

A CIP catalogue for this book is available from the British Library.

ISBN 978 1 78739 290 8

Printed in Dubai

10 9 8 7 6 5 4

CONTENTS

1
EDUCATION

Among the issues Michelle Obama worked for while First Lady, one of the closest to her heart was education. Neither of her parents went to college, but they instilled in her a respect for learning that enabled her to follow her dreams to two of the US's most prestigious universities, Princeton and Harvard, and eventually the White House. It's no wonder she believes education is the key to progress not just for young people, and especially girls, but for countries as a whole.

66

For me, education has never been
simply a policy issue – it's personal.

99

Column for CNN, October 2016

"

Neither of my parents and hardly anyone in the neighborhood where I grew up went to college. But, thanks to a lot of hard work and plenty of financial aid, I had the opportunity to attend some of the finest universities in this country. **"**

Column for CNN, October 2016

"

Empower yourself with a good education. Then get out there and use that education to build a country worthy of your boundless promise.

"

The Reach Higher Initiative
farewell speech, January 2017

❝

If my future were determined just by my performance on a standardized test, I wouldn't be here. I guarantee you that. **❞**

Campaign rally, Madison,
Wisconsin, February 2018

66

Education is the single most
important civil rights issue that we
face today.

99

Black History Month event
"Celebrating Women of the Civil Rights Movement",
February 2015

"
With an education … you have
everything you need to rise above
all the noise and fulfil every last one
of your dreams. **"**

Mulberry School for Girls Skype conversation,
London, June 2015

66

Every single child has boundless promise, no matter who they are, where they come from, or how much money their parents have. We've got to remember that. 99

National Arts and Humanities
Youth Programme awards, November 2016

" We cannot tolerate millions and millions of girls being denied the access to improve themselves and the lives of their families by being essentially locked out of the education process. **"**

Glamour magazine's "A Brighter Future: A Global Conversation on Girls' Education" event, October 2016

66

When girls are educated, their
countries become stronger and
more prosperous. **99**

FLOTUS travel journal,
Dakar, Senegal, June 2013

66

All of these young people have some kind of potential in them. And if we don't invest in them as a nation – regardless of where they come from or what colour they are – if we don't invest in them, we lose. **99**

National Arts and Humanities
Youth Programme awards, November 2016

"

One of the things that was a great fortune to me was that my parents understood the value of an education. And they fought for me, they sacrificed, they saved. **"**

Let Girls Learn event,
Marrakesh, Morocco, June 2016

66

The one thing people can't take
away from you is your education.
And it is worth the investment. **99**

National Arts and Humanities
Youth Programme awards, November 2016

"

Through my education, I didn't
just develop skills, I didn't just
develop the ability to learn, but
I developed confidence. **"**

Glamour magazine's "A Brighter Future:
A Global Conversation on Girls' Education" event,
October 2016

"
I never cut class. I loved getting As. I liked being smart. I liked being on time. I thought being smart is cooler than anything in the world. **"**

Elizabeth Garrett Anderson School,
London, April 2009

❝
For me, education was power.
❞

Column for CNN, October 2016

66 Girls know that education is their only path to self-sufficiency. It is their only chance to shape their own fate rather than having the limits of their lives dictated to them by others. **99**

Let Girls Learn event,
Washington D.C., March 2016

"

The ability to read, write, and analyze; the confidence to stand up and demand justice and equality; the qualifications and connections to get your foot in that door and take your seat at that table – all of that starts with education. **"**

Let Girls Learn Event celebrating International Women's Day, March 2016

66

I know that there are so many kids
out there just like me — kids who
have a world of potential, but
maybe their parents never went to
college or maybe they've never
been encouraged to believe they
could succeed there. **99**

College Opportunity summit,
January 2014

66

If we're always shining the spotlight
on professional athletes or recording
artists or Hollywood celebrities,
if those are the only achievements
we celebrate, then why would we
ever think kids would see college
as a priority?
99

The Reach Higher Initiative
farewell speech, January 2017

66

We can't afford not to educate girls and give women the power and the access that they need. **99**

Mulberry School for Girls Skype conversation, London, June 2015

"

If you always just go for the
grade, sometimes you'll bypass
what's interesting. **"**

Elizabeth Garrett Anderson School,
London, April 2009

66

Focus more on learning than succeeding – instead of pretending that you understand something when you don't, just raise your hand and ask a question.

99

People magazine essay,
October 2014

2
EQUALITY

As a black woman from a working class background, Michelle Obama had to forge a path through sometimes prejudiced and often intimidating environments to achieve her goals. With the platform that being First Lady afforded her, she has encouraged people to see the strength in diversity and feel empowered in the face of inequalities.

66

The difference between a broken community and a thriving one is the presence of women who are valued, where relationships among women and between women and men are based upon mutual respect. **99**

State Department Women of
Courage Awards, March 2009

66

No country can ever truly flourish if it stifles the potential of its women and deprives itself of the contributions of half its citizens. **99**

Mandela Washington Fellowship
for Young African Leaders summit, July 2014

"

Strong men, men who are truly role models, don't need to put down women to make themselves feel powerful.

"

Campaign rally, Southern New Hampshire University, October 2016

66

You see, our glorious diversity – our diversity of faiths, and colors, and creeds – that is not a threat to who we are; it makes us who we are.

99

The Reach Higher Initiative
farewell speech, January 2017

66

Like I tell my daughters, women and girls can do whatever they want. There is no limit to what we as women can accomplish. **99**

Twitter Q&A, May 2012

"

It is so important to remember that our diversity has been – and will always be – our greatest source of strength and pride. **"**

Annual Nowruz celebration,
the White House, April 2016

66

It's easier to hold onto your own
stereotypes and misconceptions;
it makes you feel justified in your
own ignorance. **99**

University of South Carolina,
March 2008

66

As long as we stay engaged and we keep empowering women, I have no doubt that we will see a woman in the Oval Office very soon. **99**

Twitter Q&A, May 2012

66

One thing that I've learned from male role models is that they don't hesitate to invest in themselves. **99**

Glamour magazine interview,
October 2009

66

Young people, particularly our girls, need to understand that doctors and scientists are something that anyone can become, no matter how much money your family has, no matter where you came from or whether you are a man or a woman. 99

National Science Foundation,
September 2011

66

Often when men are assertive or argumentative at work, they're viewed as strong and powerful. But women who act that way aren't always viewed so positively. **99**

Let Girls Learn event,
Madrid, Spain, June 2016

66

Inequalities aren't just bad for women, they're bad for men too. So many men want to be good fathers. They want to spend more time with their kids. They want their daughters to have the same opportunities as their sons. But they often find themselves powerless to shift these expectations.

99

Let Girls Learn event,
Madrid, Spain, June 2016

66

If we aren't empowering and providing the skills and the resources to half of our population, then we're not realizing our full potential as a society, as mankind. **99**

Let Girls Learn event,
Marrakesh, Morocco, June 2016

66

Women and girls who are out
there working, they are truly
force multipliers, spreading
opportunity through their families
and communities – and not just by
creating programs and nonprofit
organizations, not just by hiring other
women, but also by serving as role
models themselves.

99

The United State of Women Summit
dinner, Washington D.C., June 2016

66

The realities are that, you know, as a black man, Barack can get shot going to the gas station. **99**

60 Minutes interview,
February 2007

66

What I notice about men, all men, is that their order is: me, my family, God is in there somewhere; but me is first. And for women, me is fourth, and that's not healthy.

99

Chicago Tribune interview, September 2004

“

When you encounter folks who still hold the old prejudices because they've only been around folks like themselves, when you meet folks who think they know all the answers because they've never heard any other viewpoints, it's up to you to help them see things differently. **”**

Topeka School District Senior
Recognition Day, Kansas, May 2014

66

I am an example of what is possible
when girls from the very beginning
of their lives are loved and nurtured
by people around them.   **99**

Elizabeth Garrett Anderson School,
London, April 2009

66

When you've worked hard and
done well and walked through
that doorway of opportunity, you
do not slam it shut behind you. You
reach back and you give other folks
the same chances that helped
you succeed.

99

Democratic National Convention,
September 2012

66
No matter what, you give everybody a fair shake, and when somebody needs a hand, you offer yours. **99**

Eastern Kentucky University commencement, May 2013

66

We shouldn't be sending messages
to girls that there are things they
can't do – because there's nothing
that a girl can't do.

99

The Guardian interview,
17 November 2018

" The thing that I want you all to remember: please, please, don't base your vote, this time, on fear. Base it on possibility. Think. Listen. The game of politics is to make you afraid so that you don't think. **"**

Campaign rally, Des Moines,
Iowa, August 2007

3
FAMILY & RELATIONSHIPS

As First Lady, Michelle Obama was half of one of the world's most famous marriages and one of its most prominent mothers. But beyond these most important relationships, she has shown an understanding of and joy in connecting with other people that shines through in both her formal work and her natural candidness.

66

Barack and I were both raised by families who didn't have much in the way of money or material possessions but who had given us something far more valuable – their unconditional love, their unflinching sacrifice and the chance to go places they had never imagined for themselves. 99

Democratic National Convention,
September 2012

66

When times get tough and fear sets in, think of those people who paved the way for you and those who are counting on you to pave the way for them. **99**

University of California, Merced, commencement, May 2009

66

I call myself mom-in-chief not because
I don't value my career or education
… but the most important thing to me
is raising strong women because that's
what my mother did for me. **99**

Elizabeth Garrett Anderson School,
London, April 2009

"
With every word we utter, with every action we take, we know our kids are watching us. We as parents are their most important role models. **"**

Democratic National Convention,
July 2016

66

My mother's love has always been
a sustaining force for our family, and
one of my greatest joys is seeing
her integrity, her compassion, her
intelligence reflected in my daughters.

99

Democratic National Convention,
August 2008

"

I love our daughters more than anything in the world, more than life itself. And while that may not be the first thing that some folks want to hear from an Ivy-League-educated lawyer, it is truly who I am. **"**

Tuskegee University commencement,
Alabama, May 2015

"

Throughout my twenties and early thirties, I had jobs that I loved. I worked in city government. I ran a youth organization. I served as an associate dean at a university. And I couldn't imagine how a baby would fit into all of that. **"**

Let Girls Learn event,
Madrid, Spain, June 2016

66

I will never forget that winter morning as I watched our girls, just seven and ten years old, pile into those black SUVs with all those big men with guns.

99

Democratic National Convention,
July 2016

"

I remember one parent-teacher conference at the lower school, and Barack went, and there were SWAT guys on top of the roof of the school. And Malia was like, 'Dad, really? Really? Do they really have to be up there?' And it's like, yeah, honey, they do.

"

Legacies of America's First Ladies conference, Washington D.C., September 2016

"

The minute I graduated, suddenly everyone was asking me, 'Well, when are you going to get married and start having kids?' And the truth is I had no idea how I would balance the expected role of wife and mother with a challenging career. **"**

Let Girls Learn event,
Madrid, Spain, June 2016

66

When a father puts in long hours at work, he's praised for being dedicated and ambitious. But when a mother stays late at the office, she's sometimes accused of being selfish, neglecting her kids. **99**

Let Girls Learn event,
Madrid, Spain, June 2016

"

While I believed deeply in my husband's vision for this country – and I was certain he would make an extraordinary President – like any mother, I was worried about what it would mean for our girls. How would we keep them grounded under the glare of the national spotlight? **"**

Democratic National Convention, September 2012

66

Do not bring people in your
life who weigh you down,
and trust your instincts.

Elizabeth Garrett Anderson School,
London, April 2009

66

Good relationships feel good. They feel right. They don't hurt. They're not painful. That's not just with somebody you want to marry, but it's with the friends you choose. It's with the people you surround yourself with.

99

Elizabeth Garrett Anderson School,
London, April 2009

"

We should always have three friends in our lives: one who walks ahead who we look up to and follow; one who walks beside us, who is with us every step of our journey; and then, one who we reach back for and bring along after we've cleared the way.

"

National Mentoring Summit, Washington, DC, January 2011

"

Walk away from 'friendships' that make you feel small and insecure, and seek out people who inspire you and support you.

"

People magazine essay,
October 2014

66

You don't want to be with a boy who is too stupid to appreciate a smart young lady. There is no boy who is cute enough or interesting enough to stop you from getting your education.

99

The Power of an Educated Girl event,
New York City, September 2015

" Don't look at the bankbook or the title. Look at the heart. Look at the soul. Look at how the guy treats his mother and what he says about women. How he acts with children he doesn't know. And, more important, how does he treat you. **"**

Glamour magazine interview, October 2009

66

When you are dating a man, you should always feel good. You should never feel less than. You should never doubt yourself. **99**

Glamour magazine interview,
October 2009

"

My most important title is 'mom-in-chief'. My daughters are still the heart of my heart and the centre of my world.

"

Democratic National Convention,
September 2012

66

I started thinking about exercise as an investment in myself instead of a chore, and I started focusing on the example I wanted to set for my girls.

99

Women's Health magazine,
May 2012

66

I wake up every morning in a house that was built by slaves. And I watch my daughters, two beautiful intelligent black young women, play with the dog on the White House lawn. **99**

Democratic National Convention,
July 2016

66

I love that, for Barack, there is no such thing as 'us' and 'them' – he doesn't care whether you're a Democrat, a Republican, or none of the above … He's always looking for the very best in everyone he meets.

99

Democratic National Convention, September, 2012

"

You have to fill your bucket with positive energy and if people are bringing you down — whether that's your boo or your best friend — you have to learn how to push these people to the side. **"**

The Power of an Educated Girl event,
New York City, September 2015

66

I always tell young girls, surround yourself with goodness. I learned early on how to get the haters out of my life.

99

The United State of Women Summit
interview with Oprah Winfrey, June 2016

66

Choose people who lift you up. Find
people who will make you better.

99

ABC News interview with David Muir,
June 2011

"

Exercise is really important to me; it's therapeutic. So if I'm ever feeling tense or stressed or like I'm about to have a meltdown, I'll put on my iPod and head to the gym or out on a bike ride along Lake Michigan with the girls. **"**

Marie Claire magazine interview, October 2008

"

What makes life truly rich are the people you share it with. If you're in a fight with someone, make up. If you're holding a grudge, let it go. If you hurt someone, apologize. If you love someone, let them know. **"**

Oregon State University
commencement, June 2012

66

Don't just tell people that you love them – show them. And that means showing up. It means being truly present in the lives of the people you care about. **99**

Oregon State University commencement, June 2012

66

Women in particular need to keep an eye on their physical and mental health because … we don't have a lot of time to take care of ourselves. We need to do a better job of putting ourselves higher on our own to-do list. 99

Real Health magazine interview,
November 2007

66

Those holes we all have in our hearts are what truly connect us to each other. They are the spaces we can make for other people's sorrow and pain, as well as their joy and their love, so that eventually, instead of feeling empty, our hearts feel even bigger and fuller.

99

Dr Martin Luther King Jr High School commencement, Georgia, June 2015

❝

If you do not take control over your
time and your life, other people will
gobble it up. If you don't prioritize
yourself, you constantly start falling
lower and lower on your list, your
kids fall lower and lower on your list.

❞

The United State of Women Summit
interview with Oprah Winfrey, June 2016

4
POLITICS

Michelle Obama gave up a lucrative career as a lawyer to work in public administration and the non-profit sector, so that she could make a difference and make change. In her role as First Lady, she was clear in voicing her motivations and following her beliefs, and encouraged others to do the same, in their lives and at the ballot box.

66

I'm asking you to stop settling for the world as it is, and to help us make the world as it should be. **99**

Campaign rally, Orangeburg,
South Carolina, November 2007

"
True leadership often happens
with the smallest acts, in the most
unexpected places, by the most
unlikely individuals. **"**

Young African Women Leaders forum,
Soweto, South Africa, June 2011

66

At the end of the day, when it comes
time to make that decision, as
president, all you have to guide you
are your values, and your vision and
the life experiences that make you
who you are.   **99**

Democratic National Convention,
September 2012

"

The arts are not just a nice thing to have … Rather, paintings and poetry, music and fashion, design and dialogue, they all define who we are as a people and provide an account of our history for the next generation.

"

Metropolitan Museum of Art
American Wing opening, May 2009

66

Real change comes from
having enough comfort to
be really honest and say
something very uncomfortable. **99**

New York Times profile, June 2008

66 What I have never been afraid of is to be a little silly, and you can engage people that way. My view is, first you get them to laugh, then you get them to listen. **99**

Variety magazine interview,
August 2016

66

Elections aren't just about who
votes but who doesn't vote.

99

Campaign rally,
Virginia, September 2016

66

There are still many causes worth sacrificing for, so much history yet to be made. **99**

Young African Women Leaders forum, Soweto, South Africa, June 2011

" If you want to have a say in your community, if you truly want the power to control your own destiny, then you've got to be involved. You got to be at the table. You've got to vote, vote, vote, vote. **"**

Tuskegee University commencement, Alabama, May 2015

66

There are times when you need to
be loud and speak your mind. I've
had to do that in every room of
power that I've sat in, and I've had
to learn that my voice has value.
And if I don't use it, what's the point
of me being in the room?

99

Glamour magazine's "A Brighter Future:
A Global Conversation on Girls' Education" event,
October 2016

66

Barack knows the American Dream because he's lived it, and he wants everyone in this country to have that same opportunity, no matter who we are or where we're from or what we look like or who we love. **99**

Democratic National Convention,
September 2012

66 I have seen how leaders rule by intimidation. Leaders who demonize and dehumanize entire groups of people often do so because they have nothing else to offer. **99**

City College of New York
commencement, June 2016

66

I have seen how places that stifle the
voices and dismiss the potential of
their citizens are diminished; how they
are less vital, less hopeful, less free.

99

City College of New York
commencement, June 2016

66

I could have spent eight years doing anything, and at some level, it would have been fine. Because any First Lady, rightfully, gets to define her role. There's no legislative authority; you're not elected. And that's a wonderful gift of freedom.

99

Vogue magazine interview,
December 2016

66

Whether we're Democrats,
Republicans or independent – it
does not matter. We all understand
that an attack on any one of us
is an attack on all of us.   **99**

Campaign rally, Phoenix,
Arizona, October 2016

66

It is not about voting for the perfect
candidate – there is no such person.

99

Campaign rally, Philadelphia,
Pennsylvania, September 2016

66

I specifically did not read other First Ladies' books, because I didn't want to be influenced by how they defined the role. I knew that I would have to find this role – very uniquely and specifically to me and who I was.

99

The United State of Women Summit
interview with Oprah Winfrey, June 2016

66

I've seen how the issues that come across a president's desk are always the hard ones — the problems where no amount of data or numbers will get you to the right answer. **99**

Democratic National Convention,
September 2012

66

I think our democracy has it exactly right: two terms, eight years. It's enough. Because it's important to have one foot in reality when you have access to this kind of power.

99

Vogue magazine interview, December 2016

66
You can't make decisions based
on fear and the possibility of what
might happen. **99**

60 Minutes interview,
February 2007

"

We know that our greatness comes from when we appreciate each other's strengths, when we learn from each other, when we lean on each other.

"

City College of New York
commencement, June 2016

66

Every day, you have the power to choose our better history – by opening your hearts and minds, by speaking up for what you know is right. 99

Topeka School District Senior
Recognition Day, Kansas, May 2014

"

You will not always be able to solve
all of the world's problems at once,
but don't ever underestimate the
importance you can have. Because
history has shown us that courage
can be contagious and hope can
take on a life of its own. **"**

Young African Women Leaders forum,
Soweto, South Africa, June 2011

66

Being president doesn't change who
you are – it reveals who you are. **99**

Democratic National Convention,
September 2012

66

I left the practice of law to go into
public service for selfish reasons.
I wanted to be happy and feel
good every single day. I wanted to
wake up inspired and ready to do
something greater than myself. **99**

The United State of Women Summit
interview with Oprah Winfrey, June 2016

66

When someone's cruel or acts like a
bully, you don't stoop to their level …
When they go low, we go high. **99**

Democratic National Convention,
July 2016

"
You don't come up with the right answer if everyone at the table looks the same and thinks the same and has the same experience. **"**

White House screening of *Hidden Figures*, December 2016

66

I want to urge you to actively seek out the most contentious, polarized, gridlocked places you can find. Because so often, throughout our history, those have been the places where progress really happens – the places where minds are changed, lives transformed.

99

Oberlin College commencement,
Ohio, May 2015

"

The biggest, most dramatic change happens incrementally, little by little, through compromises and adjustments over years and decades. **"**

Oberlin College commencement,
Ohio, May 2015

66

When crisis hits, we don't turn against each other. No, we listen to each other, we lean on each other, because we are always stronger together. **99**

Democratic National Convention,
July 2016

"

We cannot sit back and hope that everything works out for the best. We cannot afford to be tired or frustrated or cynical. **"**

Democratic National Convention,
July 2016

66

When we only talk to people who think like we do, we just get more stuck in our ways, more divided, and it gets harder to come together for a common purpose. **99**

Eastern Kentucky University
commencement, May 2013

5

SELF-BELIEF

She may have become an icon as First Lady of the United States, but Michelle Obama – like many women – knows what it's like to be told that you're not enough, and that you want too much. So what's the antidote to other people's underestimations and obstructions? Believing in yourself, your worth and your potential – and getting on with being you.

"

There are a lot of people who will try to step on your confidence based on their assumptions about who they think you are. And what you have to remember is that you are competent and capable and able to do it. **"**

Howard University commencement, Washington D.C., September 2016

66

You've got to make choices that make sense for you because there's always going to be somebody who'll think you should do something differently.

99

Time magazine interview,
May 2009

66

When I hear about negative and
false attacks, I really don't invest any
energy in them, because I know who
I am. **99**

Marie Claire magazine interview,
October 2008

66

If I could give my younger self just one piece of advice: Stop being so afraid! That's really what strikes me when I look back – the sheer amount of time I spent tangled up in fears and doubts that were entirely of my own creation.

99

People magazine essay,
October 2014

"

Having your feelings hurt, having people say things about you that aren't true. Life hits you, so … you learn how to protect yourself in it. You learn to take in what you need and get rid of the stuff that's clearly not true.

"

Oprah Winfrey interview,
December 2016

66

I believe that girl power is about being the very best version of who you are. It's about developing every talent, every skill and every last bit of brain power that you have. **99**

Seventeen magazine video,
April 2014

"

Black women are hobbled by their strength and directness. I admit it: I am louder than the average human being and have no fear of speaking my mind. These traits don't come from the colour of my skin but from an unwavering belief in my own intelligence. **"**

Newsweek magazine interview,
February 2008

66

When you are struggling and you start thinking about giving up, I want you to remember something ... and that is the power of hope. The belief that something better is always possible if you're willing to work for it and fight for it.

99

Final speech as First Lady of the United States, January 2017

"

Throughout this journey, I have learned to block everything out and focus on my truth. I had to answer some basic questions for myself: Who am I? No, really, who am I? What do I care about? **"**

Tuskegee University commencement, Alabama, May 2015

"

As women and girls, we are haunted by the voices of other people who tell us what we can't do. It's something that you have to work on every single day. Every woman you know is working on this. I am still working on it.

"

Glamour magazine's "A Brighter Future: A Global Conversation on Girls' Education" event, October 2016

66

Aggressive is assertive. Loud is confidence. It's how you take those words. Maybe they were said to you, or about you, in a negative light, but you turn them around and you make them positive attributes.

99

Glamour magazine's "A Brighter Future: A Global Conversation on Girls' Education" event, October 2016

66

Remember who you always were, where you came from, who your parents were, how they raised you. Because that authentic self is going to follow you all through life, so make sure that it's solid, so it's something that you can hold on and be proud of. **99**

Howard University commencement,
Washington D.C., September 2016

"

When it comes to social media, there are just times I turn off the world. You can't be reading all that stuff. I mean, that's like letting somebody just walk up and slap you. **"**

The United State of Women Summit interview with Oprah Winfrey, June 2016

"

Don't wait for somebody to come
along and tell you you're special.

"

Vogue magazine interview,
December 2016

66

For all of you sitting here with those
doubts in your head – ignore them.
Brush them off. And just do the work.
Do the work. And it's the doing of
the work that gets you through. It's
not what other people think of you.

99

Howard University commencement,
Washington D.C., September 2016

66

I have learned that as long as I hold fast to my beliefs and values – and follow my own moral compass – then the only expectations I need to live up to are my own. **99**

Tuskegee University commencement, Alabama, May 2015

66

We as women, we have to
understand that we know more, just
even instinctively, than we think we do.

99

R.S. Caulfield School, Unification Town,
Liberia, June 2016

" [My grandfather] taught me that my destiny had not been written before I was born — that my destiny was in my hands. **"**

Campaign rally, Orangeburg, South Carolina, November 2007

"

That gnawing sense of self-doubt that is common within all of us is a lie. It's just in our heads. Nine times out of ten, we are more ready and more prepared than we could ever know.

"

Campaign rally, Orangeburg,
South Carolina, November 2007

66

Whether you come from a council estate or a country estate, your success will be determined by your own confidence and fortitude. It won't be easy, that's for sure, but you have everything you need. **99**

Elizabeth Garrett Anderson School,
London, April 2009

66

Just try new things. Don't be afraid.
Step out of your comfort zones and
soar, all right?

99

Howard University commencement,
Washington D.C., September 2016

66

No matter what struggles or setbacks you face in your life, focus on what you have, not on what you're missing.

99

Oregon State University
commencement, June 2012

❝

You have to believe in you first. Because people will try to tear you down, I guarantee you that. **❞**

White House screening of *Hidden Figures*, December 2016

"

In those darkest moments, you will have a choice: do you dwell on everything you've lost, or do you focus on what you still have and find a way to move forward with passion, with determination, and with joy?

"

Oregon State University commencement, June 2012

"

As women and young girls, we have to invest that time in getting to understand who we are and liking who we are. Because I like me. I've liked me for a very long time … But you've got to work to get to that place. **"**

The United State of Women Summit interview with Oprah Winfrey, June 2016

66

In every interaction I have had
with anybody who's had some
connection with me, I have tried to
be authentically myself. And in order
to do that, I learned that I have to do
things that I authentically care about.

99

The United State of Women Summit
interview with Oprah Winfrey, June 2016

"

It does not matter what you look like, it doesn't matter how much money your parents have – none of that matters. Skin colour, gender is the most ridiculous defining trait that we cling to. What matters is that you believe in your own potential. **"**

White House screening of
Hidden Figures, December 2016

66

I want our young people to know
that they matter, that they belong.
So don't be afraid — you hear me,
young people? Don't be afraid. Be
focused. Be determined. Be hopeful.
Be empowered.

99

The Reach Higher Initiative
farewell speech, January 2017

"
You don't have to be somebody different to be important. You're important in your own right. **"**

R.S. Caulfield School, Unification Town, Liberia, June 2016

66

A sure path to self-confidence involves
recognizing that what we often
interpret as weaknesses can actually
be some of our greatest strengths. **99**

The Guardian interview,
17 November 2018

"

Do not ever let anyone make you feel like you don't matter ... because you do. And you have a right to be exactly who you are. **"**

The Reach Higher Initiative
farewell speech, January 2017

66

That's what it means to be your true self – it means looking inside yourself and being honest about what you truly enjoy doing.

99

Oregon State University
commencement, 2012

6
SUCCESS

It's hard to imagine that someone as successful and accomplished as Michelle Obama experiences doubts and failures. But the former First Lady readily admits she's had to dig deep to find courage in moments of fear and keep persisting when it's all gone wrong. She knows there's no magic path to success – it comes from knowing who you are and what you want, then working hard to get it.

66

Success is not about the background
you are from; it is about the
confidence that you have and the
effort you are willing to invest. **99**

Elizabeth Garrett Anderson School,
London, April 2009

66

All throughout my life there are people who have underestimated me, as I'm sure they underestimate you … I always use that as a challenge. The one way to get me to work my hardest was to doubt me. **99**

Glamour magazine's "A Brighter Future: A Global Conversation on Girls' Education" event, October 2016

"

If you understand that getting help
isn't a sign of weakness but a sign of
strength, then I guarantee you that you
will get what you need to succeed.

"

Dr Martin Luther King Jr High School
commencement, June 2015

66

Stop trying to be someone who
will impress everyone else, and just
focus on being and becoming fully,
sincerely, and passionately yourself.

99

People magazine essay,
October 2014

66

One of the lessons that I grew up with was to always stay true to yourself, and never let what somebody else says distract you from your goals. **99**

Marie Claire magazine interview, October 2008

"

Being a healthy woman isn't about getting on a scale or measuring your waistline – and we can't afford to think that way. Instead, we need to start focusing on what matters – on how we feel, and how we feel about ourselves.

"

Women's Health magazine,
May 2012

66

Lead by example with hope,
never fear.

99

The Reach Higher Initiative
farewell speech, January 2017

66

No matter what negativity you hear, there is always some ray of positive hope out there that you can choose to take in. **99**

White House screening of
Hidden Figures, December 2016

66

We learned about honesty and integrity – that the truth matters … that you don't take shortcuts or play by your own set of rules … and success doesn't count unless you earn it fair and square. **99**

Democratic National Convention,
September 2012

66

We learned about dignity and decency – that how hard you work matters more than how much you make… that helping others means more than just getting ahead yourself.

99

Democratic National Convention,
September 2012

66

We learned about gratitude and humility – that so many people had a hand in our success, from the teachers who inspired us to the janitors who kept our school clean … and we were taught to value everyone's contribution and treat everyone with respect. **99**

Democratic National Convention,
September 2012

"
Other people told me that I might not be able to do well in school, for whatever reason. I was always a good student, I worked hard, but I thought there was some magic that happened … I didn't know that it was just plain old hard work. **"**

Elizabeth Garrett Anderson School,
London, April 2009

❝

What matters are the true friends you make, the activities you throw yourself into, the books you read, the skills and knowledge you acquire. Those experiences – the ones that make you stronger, smarter, and braver – are what really matter. **❞**

People magazine essay,
October 2014

“
Don't be afraid to fail. Don't be afraid to take risks. Learn to use your voice now. Ask questions. Ask stupid questions. Don't be afraid to trip, fall, and don't be afraid to get back up.

”

Elizabeth Garrett Anderson School,
London, April 2009

66

Failure is an important part of your growth and developing resilience.

99

The Power of an Educated Girl event,
New York City, September 2015

❝

I was not raised with wealth or resources … my brother and I were raised with all you really need: love, strong values and a belief that, with a good education and a whole lot of hard work, there was nothing that we could not do. **❞**

Elizabeth Garrett Anderson School,
London, April 2009

66

You should never view your challenges
as a disadvantage. Instead, it's
important for you to understand
that your experience facing and
overcoming adversity is actually one
of your biggest advantages. 99

City College of New York
commencement, June 2016

“
People who are truly strong lift others up. People who are truly powerful bring others together. **”**

Campaign rally, Manchester,
New Hampshire, October 2016

66

Do not be afraid to ask for help.
I cannot stress that enough. **99**

Dr Martin Luther King Jr High School
commencement, Georgia, June 2015

66

Nothing in my life ever would have predicted that I would be standing here as the first African-American First Lady.

Elizabeth Garrett Anderson School,
London, April 2009

"

Instead of letting your hardships and failures discourage or exhaust you, let them inspire you. Let them make you even hungrier to succeed. **"**

Dr Martin Luther King Jr High School commencement, Georgia, June 2015

66

The only limit to the height of your achievements is the reach of your dreams and your willingness to work hard for them. **99**

Democratic National Convention,
August 2008

" For heaven's sake, let yourself really fail once in a while – not some tiny little mistakes here and there, but big, glaring, confidence-shaking, dark-night-of-the-soul-inducing failures. **"**

People magazine essay,
October 2014

"

Funny thing – the more I achieved, the more I found that I was just as ready, just as qualified, just as capable as those who felt entitled to the seat at the table that I was working so hard for. **"**

Campaign rally, Orangeburg, South Carolina, November 2007

66

Success isn't about how much money
you make, it's about the difference
you make in people's lives. **99**

Democratic National Convention,
September 2012

66

You will never be happy plodding
through someone else's idea of
success. Success is only meaningful
– and enjoyable – if it feels like
your own.

99

Oregon State University
commencement, June 2012

"

Understand that no one – especially folks who are truly successful – simply coasts from achievement to achievement. The most accomplished people in the world fail and fail big. That's how they learn so much and grow so quickly and become so interesting and wise.

"

People magazine essay,
October 2014

"

The true measure of your success [is] not how well you do when you're healthy and happy and everything is going according to plan, but what do you do when life knocks you to the ground and all your plans go right out the window. **"**

Oregon State University
commencement, June 2012

"

If you're compromising through one phase of your journey, you're not giving it all up – you're compromising for that phase. There's another phase that's coming up where you might be able to have more of what you thought you wanted.

"

The United State of Women Summit
interview with Oprah Winfrey, June 2016

"

I've had to learn how to be okay with failure. Because you don't do anything great unless you're willing to fail, and then overcome the things that happen when you fail. **"**

R.S. Caulfield School, Unification Town, Liberia, June 2016

66

Being successful isn't about being impressive, it's about being inspired.

Oregon State University
commencement, 2012

99

"

Becoming is an ongoing process, a constant reaching toward a better self. It's the idea that there's always more growing to be done.

"

The Guardian interview,
17 November 2018

66

Every scar you have is a reminder
not just that you got hurt, but that
you survived … It's okay to feel the
sadness and the grief that comes
with those losses. But instead of
letting those feelings defeat you, let
them motivate you. Let them serve as
fuel for your journey. **99**

Dr Martin Luther King Jr High School
commencement, Georgia, June 2015

66

If your family doesn't have much money, I want you to remember that in this country, plenty of folks, including me and my husband — we started out with very little. But with a lot of hard work and a good education, anything is possible — even becoming president. **99**

The Reach Higher Initiative
farewell speech, January 2017

66

Doubts don't go away. You just learn how to deal with them. You start knowing yourself and you become more confident the more successes you have, the more chances you take. You don't let the failures or the stumbles define you. **99**

Elizabeth Garrett Anderson School, London, April 2009

"

You don't have to say anything to the haters. You don't have to acknowledge them at all. You just wake up every morning and be the best you you can be. And that tends to shut them up. **"**

The United State of Women Summit interview with Oprah Winfrey, June 2016

"

Success isn't about how your life looks to others, it's about how it feels to you. **"**

Oregon State University
commencement, 2012